For Vanessa & Harrison - My sweet children who inspire me to share the Good News every day. You remind me that God's generous gift of salvation is for even the littlest ones. May you understand it, accept it, and serve Him all your lives!

With special thanks to Terry Rowland.

ISBN: 978-1-7359890-0-6
Library of Congress Control Number: 2020920915
Published in Rochester, Minnesota.
Copyright © 2020 by Brooke Kashou. All rights reserved.
www.brookekashou.com

GOOD NEWS
for Me!

written by Brooke Kashou

illustrated by Sandra Herrgott

A long time ago,
God made **ALL THINGS.**

God made ME -
and He LOVES me very much!

God wants me to love
HIM, too.

Every GOOD THING that I have is from God.

"Thank you, God,
for **CARING** for me!"

The **BIBLE** tells me how to **LOVE** and **OBEY**.

God could **MAKE** me do it. But He lets me choose my **OWN WAY.**

Sometimes I **DON'T** want
to love God.
I don't want to **OBEY.**

I feel **STUBBORN** and **SELFISH.**
I only care about **ME.**

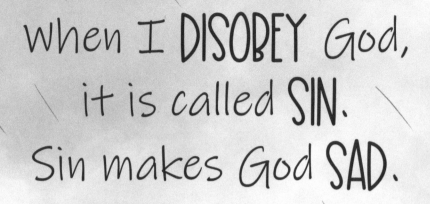

when I **DISOBEY** God,
it is called **SIN**.
Sin makes God **SAD**.

The **PUNISHMENT** for sin is death - going to a **BAD** place called Hell.

EVERYONE has sinned.
I sin every day.

But God loves me **SO MUCH**
that He made a way to
FORGIVE my sins.

God sent His son JESUS to SAVE me!

Jesus was born
as a little BABY.

Jesus grew up,
but He **NEVER** sinned.
He came to earth
so my sins could be **FORGIVEN**.

Jesus took MY punishment for sin and He DIED.

But Jesus didn't stay dead.
He came back to LIFE!

Now Jesus lives FOREVER.
And the GOOD NEWS is
that I CAN TOO!

I can live with JESUS in a wonderful place called HEAVEN.

"HOW can I do this?"

FIRST I must CONFESS my sins -
ADMIT I sin and do bad things.

Then I can REPENT -
I choose to TURN from sin.

I love Jesus SO much
that I STOP my sin and OBEY Him!

Will it be EASY?
NO!
But God will put the Holy Spirit
in my heart to HELP me.

If I **BELIEVE** Jesus died for my sins and I choose to **OBEY** and **FOLLOW** Him, that means I have **FAITH**.

The Bible says that
faith in Jesus **SAVES** me!

How do I ask God to save me from my sins? I can PRAY!

Dear God,

Please FORGIVE me for my sins.

Thank you for sending Jesus to die to take MY punishment.

Please help me to LOVE and OBEY you every day.

Thank you for loving me SO much.

Amen.

GOD MADE ALL THINGS - JOHN 1:1-3

In the beginning was the Word, and the Word was with God, and the Word was God. He was in the beginning with God. All things were made through him, and without him was not any thing made that was made.

GOD LOVES ME - 1 JOHN 4:16, 19

So we have come to know and to believe the love that God has for us. God is love, and whoever abides in love abides in God, and God abides in him. We love because he first loved us.

GOD WANTS ME TO LOVE HIM - MATTHEW 22:37-38

And he said to him, "You shall love the Lord your God with all your heart and with all your soul and with all your mind. This is the great and first commandment."

EVERY GOOD THING IS FROM GOD - JAMES 1:17

Every good gift and every perfect gift is from above, coming down from the Father of lights, with whom there is no variation or shadow due to change.

GOD CARES FOR ME - 1 PETER 5:6-7

Humble yourselves, therefore, under the mighty hand of God so that at the proper time he may exalt you, casting all your anxieties on him, because he cares for you.

LOVE GOD - 1 JOHN 5:3

For this is the love of God, that we keep his commandments. And his commandments are not burdensome.

OBEY GOD - 2 JOHN 1:6

And this is love, that we walk according to his commandments; this is the commandment, just as you have heard from the beginning, so that you should walk in it.

I DON'T NATURALLY LOVE GOD - EPHESIANS 6:12

For we do not wrestle against flesh and blood, but against the rulers, against the authorities, against the cosmic powers over this present darkness, against the spiritual forces of evil in the heavenly places.

I HAVE SELFISH DESIRES - GALATIANS 5:16-17

But I say, walk by the Spirit, and you will not gratify the desires of the flesh. For the desires of the flesh are against the Spirit, and the desires of the Spirit are against the flesh, for these are opposed to each other, to keep you from doing the things you want to do.

SIN MAKES GOD SAD - EPHESIANS 4:30

And do not grieve the Holy Spirit of God, by whom you were sealed for the day of redemption.

THE PUNISHMENT FOR SIN IS DEATH - ROMANS 6:23

For the wages of sin is death, but the free gift of God is eternal life in Christ Jesus our Lord.

EVERYONE HAS SINNED - ROMANS 3:23

For all have sinned and fall short of the glory of God.

GOD WANTS TO FORGIVE MY SINS - 2 PETER 3:9

The Lord is not slow to fulfill his promise as some count slowness, but is patient toward you, not wishing that any should perish, but that all should reach repentance.

JESUS CAME TO SAVE ME - JOHN 3:16-17

For God so loved the world, that he gave his only Son, that whoever believes in him should not perish but have eternal life. For God did not send his Son into the world to condemn the world, but in order that the world might be saved through him.

JESUS WAS SINLESS - HEBREWS 4:15

For we do not have a high priest who is unable to sympathize with our weaknesses, but one who in every respect has been tempted as we are, yet without sin.

JESUS TOOK MY SIN ON HIMSELF - 2 CORINTHIANS 5:21

For our sake he made him to be sin who knew no sin, so that in him we might become the righteousness of God.

JESUS DIED FOR MY SIN - 1 PETER 3:18

For Christ also suffered once for sins, the righteous for the unrighteous, that he might bring us to God, being put to death in the flesh but made alive in the spirit.

JESUS ROSE FROM THE DEAD - 1 CORINTHIANS 15:3-4

For I delivered to you as of first importance what I also received: that Christ died for our sins in accordance with the Scriptures, that he was buried, that he was raised on the third day in accordance with the Scriptures[.]

JESUS LIVES FOREVER - HEBREWS 7:24-25

But he holds his priesthood permanently, because he continues forever. Consequently, he is able to save to the uttermost those who draw near to God through him, since he always lives to make intercession for them.

I CAN LIVE FOREVER - JOHN 5:24

Truly, truly, I say to you, whoever hears my word and believes him who sent me has eternal life. He does not come into judgment, but has passed from death to life.

I CAN LIVE WITH JESUS - JOHN 14:1-3

Let not your hearts be troubled. Believe in God; believe also in me. In my Father's house are many rooms. If it were not so, would I have told you that I go to prepare a place for you? And if I go and prepare a place for you, I will come again and will take you to myself, that where I am you may be also.

I CAN GO TO HEAVEN - PHILIPPIANS 3:20-21

But our citizenship is in heaven, and from it we await a Savior, the Lord Jesus Christ, who will transform our lowly body to be like his glorious body, by the power that enables him even to subject all things to himself.

I MUST CONFESS MY SINS - 1 JOHN 1:9

If we confess our sins, he is faithful and just to forgive us our sins and to cleanse us from all unrighteousness.

I MUST REPENT - ACTS 3:19

Repent therefore, and turn back, that your sins may be blotted out[.]

I OBEY JESUS BECAUSE I LOVE HIM - JOHN 14:15

If you love me, you will keep my commandments.

THE HOLY SPIRIT HELPS ME OBEY - JOHN 14:26

But the Helper, the Holy Spirit, whom the Father will send in my name, he will teach you all things and bring to your remembrance all that I have said to you.

Romans 8:8-10 - Those who are in the flesh cannot please God. You, however, are not in the flesh but in the Spirit, if in fact the Spirit of God dwells in you. Anyone who does not have the Spirit of Christ does not belong to him. But if Christ is in you, although the body is dead because of sin, the Spirit is life because of righteousness.

FAITH IS BELIEF THAT LEADS TO OBEDIENCE - ROMANS 10:9

Because, if you confess with your mouth that Jesus is Lord and believe in your heart that God raised him from the dead, you will be saved.

James 2:26 - For as the body apart from the spirit is dead, so also faith apart from works is dead.

FAITH IN JESUS SAVES ME - EPHESIANS 2:8-9

For by grace you have been saved through faith. And this is not your own doing; it is the gift of God, not a result of works, so that no one may boast.

I CAN PRAY TO BE SAVED - ROMANS 10:13

For "everyone who calls on the name of the Lord will be saved."

CPSIA information can be obtained
at www.ICGtesting.com
Printed in the USA
LVHW071940171120
671944LV00004B/173